Strands and Ripples

Also by David Atkinson and published by Ginninderra Press
Ablation of Time

David Atkinson
Strands and Ripples

Acknowledgements

Many of the poems in this collection, some in slightly different form, have appeared in the following publications (in Australia unless shown): *Australian Poetry Collaboration*, *Avalon Literary Review* (US), *The Avocet* (US), *Backstory*, *The Blue Nib*, *Dream Catcher* (UK), *Eureka Street*, *FAWWA*, *Foxtrot Uniform* (UK), *FreeXpresSion*, *Friday Flash Fiction* (UK), *Harbour in the Window*, *Hornsby Ku-ring-gai Post*, *In Daily*, *Life is Good* (US), *Messages from the Embers*, *Monthly Chronicle*, *Mountain Secrets*, *The Mozzie*, *Northampton Poetry Review* (UK), *The Pen* (US), *Pennine Platform* (UK), *Pif* (US), *Poetry for Public Transport*, *Poetry Matters*, *Polestar*, *Positive Words*, *Quadrant*, *Scribes Writers*, *The Senior*, *Tamba*, *Time of Singing* (US), *Valley Micropress* (NZ), *Verdant Truth Serum*, *WA Poets*.

I am grateful to the editors and publishers for their encouragement of poets and their dedication to poetry.

The following poems have won awards in competitions:
'The Straining Rowlocks', 2nd, Tom Collins National Poetry Prize, 2019;
'The Light of Dawn', 2nd, Scribes Writers Poetry Competition (Traditional), 2019;
'Migration of the Bar-tailed Godwits', 1st, Scribes Writers Poetry Competition (Traditional), 2020;
'Flute Notes', Commended, Ros Spencer Poetry Prize, 2020;
'Involuntary Witness', Shortlisted, Poetry Matters Competition, 2020

Strands and Ripples
ISBN 978 1 76109 108 7
Copyright © text David Atkinson 2021
Cover image: falco from Pixabay

First published 2021 by
GINNINDERRA PRESS
PO Box 3461 Port Adelaide 5015
www.ginninderrapress.com.au

Contents

The Insistent Chords

Birthday Ballot	11
The Call of the Camembert	12
Clapping Hands	13
Nine-tenths	14
Fighting the Undertow	15
Zuckerberg's Dissident	16
Man Cave	17
Old-world Technology	18
Transformed	19
Common Cold Ambiguity	20
Ode to My Straw Hat	21

Untouched Joy

Unsealed Innocence	25
The Arc of Sharpened Steel	26
Degrees of Deception	27
Watching Television	28
The Camber of the Canter	29
Dawn Downpour	31
Clotted Clag	32
The Scents of Memory	33
Prying into the Past	35
Drawing Pins	37
Somersaults	38

The Sun-sliced Heat Haze

The Flash of Indelible Pink	41
Eco-villanelle	42
Eye Rings	43
The Grief of Mountains	44

Flute Notes	45
The Light of Dawn – a Villanelle	47
Questions in the Pre-dawn	48
The Mind of an Ornithologist	49
Man of the Frangipani	50
Standover Tactics	51
The Polarity of Mosquitoes	52
Contrasting Perspectives	53
The Conservation of Ideas	55

The Rhythmic Ripples

The Redundant Thermometer	59
The Kelpie's Chain	60
The Straining Rowlocks	61
From the Killing Tree	63
Villanelle for Archie	64
Glinting Barrels	65
A Letter to Bath	68
Colour Within Colour	69
The Curve of Her Shoulder	70
Weeping Guitar	71

Fibres of Filament

Corrugated Tymbals	75
Raptor Banquet	76
Migration of the Bar-tailed Godwits	77
Ephemeral Pelicans	78
Soldered Strands	79
Dead Tree Cycle	80
Elevated Insight	81
Fresh Flesh	82
Budding Lovers	83
Gundagai Swaths	84

A Prickly Relationship	85
Wavelets of Sound	86
Albumen Foam	87

Alone In the Azure

Legacies of the Delta	91
Rolling Gravy Mince	92
Sibling Harmony	93
Orbiting the Orb	94
Involuntary Witness	95
Sifted	96
Viewfinder	97
Contemporary Kant	98
Postmodern Communication	99
Flickering Flaneur	100
I'm a Celebrity Get Me Out of Syria	101

Beyond Plains and Canals

The Jive of Life	105
Chess Pieces	106
Mesas and Buttes	107
Collapsed Time	108
Looking for America	109
The Authority of Survival	111
An Hour at the Hermitage	112
Imagined Russia	113
Coagulated Time	115
Freight Train of the Senses	117
Resolutions For a Different Day	119

Thanks	120

For Judy

The Insistent Chords

Birthday Ballot

My eyes grapple with the diffusion of headlights,
oscillation of wipers in the downpour
and I am immersed in the insistent chords
of a guitar laden with the lyrics of Don Walker.
The alchemy of 'Khe Sanh' spirits, commandeers
me back to the early seventies.

I am transported to the sappers.
In a pitch-dark deluge like this,
gun turrets and slush banish daydreams
of beaches and cobalt rockpools.

Recollections of the birthday ballot,
tremble of black and white TV in the corner.
My fingers drag a crested envelope from the letterbox,
the afternoon breeze brings ironic coo
of peaceful doves.

Mist of defoliant invades the recess
of my imagination; a persistent aftertaste
of the jungle, the tang of perspiration.

In my speeding cocoon I mouth a prayer
of thanks for the deferral,
the abolition of national service.
Staring into the dappled darkness
I touch the pain of a generation.

The Call of the Camembert

The jukebox music throbs, thuds through the dancers.
Reverberation, dissection as if by an avalanche.
After fifty years the Stones still *can't get no satisfaction.*

The sour smell of writhing bodies, brains bounce
behind foreheads, angular arms flail like isosceles triangles.
Shaken hair cascades, cannons across the rapids

of glare-glinted headlands. Lounging guests spreadeagle
like the wounded on settees and antiquated bean bags,
the introvert veterans of earlier rock 'n' roll campaigns.

Some attempt to talk, no one tries to listen;
words drift away, a process of oral evaporation.
You can start me up, but for some the clarion call

comes not from a clarinet, not from a saxophone,
but from the platter in the corner,
duck liver pâté, the camembert.

Clapping Hands

Infant squirms, high chair animation.
Crashes his spoon, bunnykin plate percussion,
flare of the window's sun.
Hair curls bob on the swell of the fontanelle,
residual scent of bathtime.

Chomps on the mushy mouthful,
viscous mess of rice cereal.
Waves the rigidity, solidity of the spoon.
Stares at the floor tiles,
throws down the implement.
Clatter resounds through the gauze door,
clamour of clapping hands.

Physics class, a teenager,
the dreariness of school.
Eyelids droop, throb of the ceiling fan
caresses the page.
The law of universal gravitation studied,
understood at kitchen preschool.

Nine-tenths

The citrine sphere of the sun, long lashed to the horizon,
slides at last beneath the mulga, the dunes
of the town limits.

At the isolated motel, seared bank of a dry creek,
reluctant fan thrums like a council of flies
beyond the gauze; woman glances up
from sweat-soaked shoulders, pierces
the languor of the air: you must park only
in the spot numbered for your unit.

On return from the club's sirloin steak and schooner special,
designated bay has been usurped,
invaded, by a dust-covered four-wheel drive,
the driver a descendant of original inhabitants
of the remote community further west.

The sun has deserted, the moon eludes intrusion.
Bearing the weight of colonial history, the door closes,
locking out the sky, dark cobalt and tartaric.

Fighting the Undertow

For Ian H. (1925–2019)

We watch you sit, the sunshine on your face
illuminates a will now in decline;
this silent space
of frailty with your smile a cautious sign
which does not indicate, cannot define

the vibrance you have brought to many lives.
At over ninety years the dancing eyes,
the core survives,
your charity and wisdom typifies
a kindliness and all that this implies.

In retrospect your clients sign their wills,
their hardest problems brought for you to bear;
you ply your skills.
A gracious courtesy becoming rare,
for decade and then decade selfless care.

Your skin feels chilled, a beannie for the cold,
in pain and weariness the calm you know
with love consoled.
The insights ebb, your spirits now so low,
exemplar as you fight the undertow.

The spark will dim, the light and joy must fade
as languid summer days will drift and wane.
My debt unpaid,
you show me grace as cloud mists into rain
but memory and hope will still remain.

Zuckerberg's Dissident

We try to stay in touch when you're away.
Parental love runs deeper than you know
and truth be told we miss you every day.

Friends indicate that Facebook is the way
but selfie boastfulness is not our go.
We try to stay in touch when you're away.

Within our private world is where we'll stay,
attention seekers reap the crop they sow.
Now truth be told we miss you every day.

The distance to New York begins to weigh
but Instagram and Twitter we'll forego.
We try to stay in touch when you're away.

On social media a wide array
of posts and tweets to stroke the frail ego.
The truth be told we miss you every day.

There's vanity and swagger as they play
but we'll avoid the ostentatious show.
We try to stay in touch when you're away
and truth be told we miss you every day.

Man Cave

Between my finger and my thumb
The squat pen rests.
I'll dig with it.
'Digging' – Seamus Heaney (1964)

I watch the blade as the drop saw sings,
slices through the pine, the redolence,
astringency of fine sawdust.
Eyes leak, oil soaks his digits,
lubrication of precision machines.
Screech of power tools alleviated
only in part by woolly muffs.
To drill, to cut and weld.

They say that every man should have a shed
where he can undertake the labours of a man.

Reluctant to build and assemble, I dissemble,
return to the escritoire, my workshop.
My tool a fountain pen
charged with blue ink.

Old-world Technology

Tiny head trembles, whiskers twitch,
tail trails, disappears
into the dormant oil heater.
Was that a mouse?

'Something must be done.'
For so long disregarded,
languid in the drawer,
the mousetrap is retrieved.
Immobile innocence.

Spring-loaded, cold wire no longer inert,
components transformed into a machine for killing.
Golden saffron cheese, pungent,
counterbalances stained wood.

A fitful night of perhaps significant seconds.
Rises early in anticipation
to inspect the outcome,
to establish there is no need
to build a better mousetrap.

Transformed

Prescription spectacles rest, dormant concavity,
on the bedside table, approaching daybreak.
Inert assemblage of granite grey frames and screws.

Discordance of the shift workers' train drifts
through the scribbly saplings.
Sceptical sunlight penetrates the curtain,
infiltrates the room; he reaches out
to the bedside table.

His glasses, now in place, are transformed
into a precision instrument.
To fill the kettle, to stoop down the steps for the newspaper.
To explore the garden and to scout for, be transported by,
the rubine red of the king parrot.

The day has commenced with sight
and hope for insight, no longer to see
through a glass, darkly.

Common Cold Ambiguity

Do you have a cough or cold?
In the doctor's waiting room, camp for itinerants,
he joins the segregated section.

Sonorous silence. He knows that he must wait,
he is early; ignore the shadow,
the smell of solemnity.

He is aware that he should not touch the magazines;
eyes sealed, he finds himself
in an airlift of the imagination.

Why should a cough or cold be sinister?
There must be hundreds
of thousands with a seasonal cold.

The identical trucks in northern Italy
rumble in convoy to the closest available
crematoriums and morgues.

The television flickers in the corner;
he hopes he can contribute
to flattening the Bell curve.

Sorry for the delay;
the doctor will see you now.

Ode to My Straw Hat

after Pablo Neruda

Sedate, asleep as if you hibernate
beneath the car's rear window,
await the change of season,
foresee the dawn of spring.
Winter wanes, your treated straw
awakens to the warmth.

You shadow me, straw hat,
on early walks through vibrant blooms,
the balm of drifting pollens.
At surf club kiosk,
firmly pushed upon my head,
shading, gazing out to sea,
you smell with me ground coffee beans.

Some say you are inanimate,
devoid of soul, misread your role.
The morning lawn, you rally then,
soak up my perspiration.
Protect me from the burning sun,
defence against the magpie,
marauding lord of its possessive nest.

I'd hoped you would maintain your shape;
your brim distorts, convulses out of line.
Perhaps you are an anarchist, subversive.
A little bent at least.

The years go by, now creases, holes
and stains from our exertions.
You've earned your rest,
you near the end,
a useful life well lived.

Untouched Joy

Unsealed Innocence

The unsealed road deviates
from gorges and gullies, transects cuttings
to the quarry. Excavated by front-loader,
earth transported in a dump truck.
In a reverie the engineer designs and labours.
Formulates and forges an industrial estate.

The purity of dirt
on nimble fingers,
the stench of rank soil
as he concentrates,
face ruddy in the half-light.
Fixes on the russet workings.

With Tonka trucks of plastic and steel,
he perseveres to construct
the infrastructure of childhood.
Under a wooden ramp six feet square.

The Arc of Sharpened Steel

Yellow box logs are stacked,
harvest of the crosscut saw
rasping through fallen trees.

Teenager confronted by the wood heap,
challenging in the untested daylight.
You must wear protective shoes, son.
The shiny axe head, razor-edged,
complements the resting hickory,
streamlined in the palms.

Shoulders strain, he arches his back,
the wedge curves skyward.
Blade, galvanised, accelerates and drives into the grain,
retaliates through the wrists,
vibrates up his arms.

The flashing arc of sharpened steel,
tang of freshly splintered wood,
of blitzed chips and kindling.
Waves of sound, timbre of the timber,
ring across the yard.

Degrees of Deception

Exhausting day, a country drive
through starlit night, celestial calm.
Returning to the family farm,
his eyelids droop; a lad of five.

He drifts away, a formless heap,
spreadeagled on the car's backseat.
Conceives a plan, a child's deceit:
when home, pretend to be asleep.

The beating tyres a lullaby,
the boy's fatigue observed, unsaid.
Strong arms will lift him to his bed,
embrace of love, a dozing sigh.

Uncomplicated boyhood scheme,
before the guile of dirty tricks
now prevalent in politics.
A naive childhood it would seem.

Watching Television

    From the timber cottage
the earthen track leads into piercing air,
into eerie moonless black.

    Imagined predators
threaten and the young boy's face,
his skin perceives, apprehends

    the hazards
of his odyssey. A towering iceberg snarls,
motionless and forbidding: formless

    monolith of the hayshed.
The pungent Jersey cows drift as galleons
in shipping lanes, the billowing darkness.

    Shallow puddles
to be avoided by memory, by instinct.
At expedition's end the trendy

    invention in the corner
will flicker in black and white; a walk
for an episode, a morality tail

    on Ben Cartwright
and his sons in the American west.

The Camber of the Canter

i.

Before the accident you rode out every day.
Now, when you hear the avalanche of hooves,
you sink into the sanctuary of memory,

the sanctity of a riding reverie.
In the raw untested day, the tang of July,
the horse appears at the fence and nuzzles

your palm. Like a child seeking security,
she seems to seek, to ask for the bridle.
Your boots braced, you throw on the cloth

and tighten the saddle's girth, its pungent
astringency. Fist to armpit you measure the stirrups
as the chestnut prances, a ballerina keen to commence.

ii.

You always say you can judge a man by the way
he sits a trotting horse, the bump and the bounce.
You must find your seat, you flex your knees

and take the weight lightly in the irons.
The trees thrust to the early sun,
red gum redolence, a lone magpie lark

trips its way through the dew. You watch for
fallen branches; even the sure-footed can stumble.
You are aware that untouched joy can be precarious.

iii.

You lean into the breeze, a time to canter.
The mare settles into her rhythm, you adapt
to the sloping ground, the camber of the canter.

Horse and rider work and sweat as one; your flight absorbs
your being. Perhaps you cannot conquer time but
hurtling through winter's greyscape you range

beyond the outcrops of your life. As you race
across the crisp glass, time is an untamed
brumby which refuses to be broken.

iv.

Every horse has an instinct for the way home.
You are in sight of the homestead
when a shimmering blanket of sulphur-crested

cockatoos ripples from the oat stubble;
your losses and sadness, ethereal,
disperse and melt into the landscape.

Dawn Downpour

The cloudburst gusts across the lucerne,
expansive pasture soaked, seeping.
Like a ram on a rampage,
squalls through the homestead
orange trees, buds mutilated,
stripped leaves now careless mulch.

Corriedale sheep seek shelter
under weeping grey box,
fleeces like damp huddled sponges.
Hereford cattle avert their docile eyes,
rumps as ramparts against the invasion.

Sonorous stampede on the iron roof,
corrugated cacophony.
Gushing into gutters,
overflowing rusted downpipes.
Puddling on the forlorn grass,
beyond still imagined drains.

He camouflages a glance
from the coverlet
to the pale light
of the failed sunrise.
Peeks at the silk sheet veil
cascading down the crystal pane.
Woken by the deluge;
comforted, he drifts back to sleep.

Late to rise, a day of wet fleeces,
a time to work indoors in the shed,
the day's shearing abandoned.

Clotted Clag

In my boyhood home, unfledged days, two Kiewa Scheme*
workers' cottages lashed, spliced together, my mother assumes
control of the second bathroom. She is custodian of her storeroom.

The linoleum floor is covered with timber fruit boxes,
enamel bread bins, containing entangled paraphernalia
which might be needed one day.

Spare saucepans, cutlery, stretched gut tennis racquets
in their wooden presses. Framed pastoral scenes of sheep grazing
in undulating frosted paddocks.

And of red gum-lined rivers (when rivers still ran).
Newsprint and magazines are stacked by the pile;
Women's Weekly, Woman's Day, Australasian Post.

On the varnished dining table by kerosene lamp,
in the patterned shapes of half light, the silent expanse
of concentration, I apply myself to my school project

a textural sheet of white cardboard, notes gleaned
from the *Pears Cyclopaedia* copied word for word.
With care I place the pictures of Hereford cattle

extracted from a magazine located in the pile.
I daub the images with homemade glue;
'The Australian Beef Industry' now complete.

Visceral aroma, fingers immersed
in the innocence, the clotted clag
of childhood.

---

* The Kiewa Hydroelectric Scheme was constructed in the high
country of Victoria between 1938 and 1961.

The Scents of Memory

To recollect that day fifty years ago, a new year
of boarding school, recall the February train trip;
the early farewell from the farm, fragrance of lavender Yardley,
of sleepy dressing gown.

Hark back to the breezy car window,
earth road compacted, candour of freshly-baled lucerne
suspended in veiled drizzle.

At the deserted station recapture the waft of wheat from trucks,
the siding silos, symbols of town. The scent of moist lichen
and of wild dandelion, weeds shooting from concrete crevices.

Take yourself back, it seems yesterday,
dragging your suitcase into the carriage;
the dining car aroma of cooked breakfasts.

Be seated in the dog box, staleness of sleeping soldier, shoeless,
on his trip from Bonegilla to Kapooka.
Redolence of his Craven As.

Reminisce as the diesel locomotive strains, strength of the grind,
squeal of wheel, a caged track animal.
Breathe the stench of petrol fumes, idling cars waiting,
persistent level crossing bells.

Contemplate pollen powder drifting from Paterson's Curse,
mauve outspread as a blanket in gauzy sun
beyond the airy compartment.

The rebounding tang of the train
through the steep-sided cutting,
the wave of the fettlers from their trolley,
while you inhale the whiff of work.

Reflect, muse upon the late afternoon in the city.
The reek of the heat, hemmed-in footpaths,
fenced stench of the suburbs.

At day's end part of you is still standing by the doorless
booking office, cardboard mustiness of parcels and freight.
Father's reserve, handshake of gabardine
and of pressed khaki, Pears soap.
You are a man now.

Prying into the Past

The fragile envelope, yellowing,
constitutes history.
Postmarked 'Sydney: 7 Nov 1963',
'Blood donors are urgently needed',
queen's head '5d' stamp.
And the letter conveys intimacy,
missive of a marriage.

Hesitating, he unveils a narrative,
stares through a peephole
into the past.

In the Sydney autumn,
the branches unsettled,
the cadence of a breeze
at the window.
Arches her back, profile leans
to her writing, hair drapes
across her face.

Concentrates, composes, imagines.
'The telephone is so expensive.'
Communicates news of family,
hopes for the farm, family again.
Fingers caress paper,
as tactile and crisp
as starched linen.

Grandchildren would be baffled
by the formality
and by the permanence.
From the commencing 'My darling'
to the concluding 'Always yours alone',
Quink ink loops and swerves,
curls and swirls,
illuminates the correspondents.
The shades of cobalt
in the open ink bottle.

The reader encroaches,
a disconcerted intruder.
All those years later,
contemplates the day when,
in a country lane,
handwritten cursive
filters through a roadside mailbox.

Drawing Pins

The photographs of pop groups torn from *Go-Set* magazine
plaster each wall of my bedroom, the window to the veranda
the only surface spared.
Tacked, suspended on the drawing pins of the imagination,
The Searchers *walk in the room*.

An isolated cottage down a country lane,
insulated by the gauze from the restless insects
of the keen lilac night.
Tacked, suspended on the drawing pins of the imagination,
The Rolling Stones, *play with fire*.

The British bands have completed their invasion,
my immersion in the music from the radio,
the dial of daydreams.
Tacked, suspended on the drawing pins of the imagination,
The Kinks, *you really got me*.

Surrounded on the blankets by Top 40 charts of the New 2UW,
I yearn for the glamour of life as a mop top,
the adulation of long-legged girls.
Tacked, suspended on the drawing pins of the imagination,
The Animals, *it's my life*.

The Beatles Show carried on the airwaves from 4BC Brisbane
across the star-flecked sky to the Riverina.
I soar, transported to Liverpool.
Tacked, suspended on the drawing pins of the imagination.
The Beatles *in my life*.

Somersaults

Contemporary times can seem a juggernaut
of arguments and mercenary concerns;
we're challenged by the basics we were taught
of care and equity where each discerns
a useful life, a span where one narrates
a dream of hope amidst the mad debates.

My childhood was an artless simpler time;
I never thought of such complexity.
No whim beyond another tree to climb;
the only one with needs or wants was me.
A younger time of homemade catapults
and sun-filled days of naive somersaults.

The Sun-sliced Heat Haze

The Flash of Indelible Pink

…but my mind
Basks in the light I never left behind.
– *Sentenced to Life*, Clive James

In the lucerne paddock, tinge of commencing green,
a galaxy of galahs umbrellas the well-tilled soil.
The flock billows, pillows, as it rises,

reaching red and charcoal, across the expanse
of the sun-sliced heat haze. Tilts, serrates as a black
flick knife, confederated screeching in the stillness

and is gone. But endures in the memory,
enlarged to linger and recur in the flight
through the decades of the imagination.

He lives with the intensity, inhalation of endless
air, the smack of cultivated earth,
unfading clarity of swissen-like young days.

Again the flash of indelible pink pitches and swerves,
enduring bloom of the birds of the mind,
the sprawled sensory delight of childhood.

Eco-villanelle

Each day I pass this eucalyptus tree,
blanched branches soar above my morning stroll.
This giant is indispensable to me.
Destruction of this beauty means that we
would lacerate our tribe's communal soul.
Each day I pass this eucalyptus tree.
Survival of our species; we shall see
our ignorance, misunderstand our role.
This giant is indispensable to me.
To map a lasting future let's agree
that every tree's essential to the whole.
Each day I pass my eucalyptus tree.
Short sightedness and rank hypocrisy
may take this gum beyond benign control.
This giant is indispensable to me.
We mess it up we'll have nowhere to flee;
barbed chainsaws lead us to a bare dustbowl.
Each day I pass my eucalyptus tree,
it's indispensable compared to me.

Eye Rings

The superb lyrebird flaunts its feathers,
bistre plumes, a gossamer fan.
Warbles his vibrato, mimics the magpie,
trills his keynote for a mate.

Observer pursues a quest for scientific knowledge,
longs to trumpet his exhilaration
from the colony to his distant colleagues.
Obsesses about taxonomy, binomial appellation.

Aims; the gunshot rings out, reverberates
across the gorge. The stench of smoke lingers.
Another specimen cut down
in the name of scholarly research.

Generates work for his team at the stuffing table.
Sharpened scalpels, forceps and bone cutters,
gleaming in the hands. Flax and straw
immersed, preserved in camphor and arsenic.
Viscous absorption; the chemical odour, the aftertaste
of gutting and passerine gravy.

Legs are bound together, trussed in surrender.
Painstaking care. Sensitivity with the eye rings,
luminous in the half-light.

The Grief of Mountains

She watches the dappled light seep
through gums to bathe the clinging sedges,
diffuse the shrouds on disconsolate peaks.

The mourning moan of a solitary currawong
transports a hinterland of memories,
cascades through hidden silence.

The cloudscapes of imagination,
undergrowth of opportunities lost,
the melancholy of a grief in all things.

She yearns for the sunlit splash of waterfalls,
exhilaration, the vibrance of invisible heights
amid the weeping rain.

A solace from sadness, she embraces
the muted tremble, the relief of grief,
the misery of mountains.

Flute Notes

I lean back, as the evening comes on.
A chicken hawk floats over, looking for home.
I have wasted my life.
– James Wright

When I hear you whistle, your repeated king parrot
flute notes, I know that you have come to rest
in our feed tree.

When you tinkle like a glass wind chime,
the almost silent strain teased out by the breeze,
you devour the ripe seeds with quiet application,
leave the squabble to cacophonous lorikeets.
As I sit, you open me to my existence.
You launch, lift across the haze of the valley
the screech of steam train brakes, weekend excursion,
the distant pitch of an A380
on its destined descent to Mascot.

When you beat in, wayfarer on the wing,
slow and low motion, I see your meticulous scarlet splash
as you hang, acrobat not quite camouflaged in the massed greenery,
invisibly connected to your mild mate clinging, clinking nearby.
You discard used husks, dense leaves,
as you graze and scatter, polite wastrel.

I observe the variable greens of the lush bush,
the cumulus clouds drifting high beyond you,
you lead me into the shades of light.

When I inhale, concentrated detection,
the floating pollens of late spring
or the moist must of an autumn storm,
you reveal to me the frail balance of nature.
You draw my attention to dank leafiness,
to the rustle of unsettled fronds.
I am aware of the essences transported on
the long-awaited southerly at dusk,
the close of an extended January day.

When I sip the strong ochre tea steaming in the mug,
I watch your race against the light in the drooping foliage;
I taste regrets, you challenge me to consider the years spent
away from the hammock.

When the sun fades from my face,
or the misty drizzle fluffs your feathers
and I reach for a jacket as the daylight pales, I touch,
reflect upon my memories layered through the decades,
 yearn for a release from what is not important.

The Light of Dawn – a Villanelle

The trap is set, its jaws are jagged steel
beneath the fence, a much-used thoroughfare.
Perhaps you've never heard a rabbit squeal.
To kill these feral pests is the ideal;
the farm must not be ravaged bleak and bare.
The trap is set, its jaws are jagged steel.
All night the boy endeavours to conceal
imagined cries, unknowing, unaware.
Perhaps you've never heard a rabbit squeal.
The leg may break and shred, the blood congeal;
the deadly tool will dominate, ensnare.
The trap is set, its jaws are jagged steel.
The muted moon observes the grim ordeal,
protracted hours now pass into despair.
Perhaps you've never heard a rabbit squeal.
The dawn brings light sufficient to reveal
the boy has learned with diligence and care.
The trap was set, its jaws were jagged steel.
Perhaps you've never heard a rabbit squeal.

Questions in the Pre-dawn

The bedroom remains a photographer's darkroom,
beyond half gloom, but there may be light
at the edge of the curtain.

I wish I could recall the cycle of the moon.
Has the neighbour's external light been tripped
by a stray owl or an early kookaburra?
Or is dawn approaching?

Must try to slip back to oblivion…
is this contemplation? Or rumination?
Perhaps I can settle on this side…
What do I regret from yesterday?
What things were left undone?

Can I concentrate sufficiently to meditate
or will that waken me?
Can I simply be in the present;
would that be mindfulness?

Is the morning hue subdued or brighter
than it was forty minutes ago?

What time is it? Why am I in a dark place?
Should I be thinking of embracing the day?

The Mind of an Ornithologist

The long-tailed finch, spring coiled, flashes
from seeding grass to spinifex. Teet teet
as it searches and preens in the afternoon sun.

I watch its dashing dart, the breast of fawn
projecting the black bib. Across the Kimberley,
the Northern Territory, far from the waft

of the eucalypt, naturalists observe the tiny bird,
its beauty and utility, adaptation to the arid
environment, the searing sand.

I ruminate on the unique bob of the head,
stretch and retraction of the neck, on landing.
At least partly involuntary, why does it bob

and what purpose does this serve?
Perhaps descended from the history
of the courtship dance,

display of the tactile grass stem.
Speculation of the aim to minimise aggression,
a gesture of appeasement

in the action of the desert.
It is not the finch which is compelled
to understand.

Man of the Frangipani

The mattock arcs, water wheel of the air, transfer of weight
from the thickness of the thighs of the muscular man;
the spade thuds as a neat square of lawn is carved out

supplanted by a less formal square of soil, his shrub
for the nature strip. Frail roots embedded with care
in the potting mix, odour of tactile nutrient compost.

The stem supported by four steel stays.
You should remove any russet leaves
and water with restraint.

A nearby magpie carols; the young plant, burgeoning,
is caressed by salty breeze, unconscious
of its potential contribution.

The volunteer frangipani man waves, moves off
on his quest to beautify.

Standover Tactics

Invader of native gardens,
privet appears benign even benevolent;
it punches at the edges of the law, outlaw bikie gang,
the organised crime of the world of plants.

To take territory, to crowd out law abiding residents,
privet adopts, shapes the strategies
of the underworld, of the undergrowth.
Kingpins orchestrate gang violence,
ground force operatives engage in standover tactics,
the jackboot conduct of the suckers
masked by a sweet pungent scent, by the airborne pollen
of their blooms drifting on an innocent breeze.

In ornamental valleys, in dark alleys faces are shoved into the wall,
arms wrenched, twisted behind their backs.
No dickering here; the law is for sissies,
an occasional short arm jab to the guts.

Melaleuca, callistemon, prepare for
a drawn-out death by strangulation.

The Polarity of Mosquitoes

In the glowing light beneath the lab window,
researcher's eyes, penetrating as the sunrise,
focus on the screen,

relieved to start his work experience with a simple
scientific enquiry free of dilemma:
should we eradicate mosquitoes?

He reads the file *Mosquitoes: the Benefits.*
Ducks scoop and swallows swoop,
a lengthy list of birds which need, feed on the bugs.
And an extensive catalogue of fish, spiders, turtles;
in his mind he smells bats snatching mosquitoes.
Perhaps their vital role as pollinator of plants
and as a food source could not be replaced.

He skims another file *Mosquitoes: the Disaster.*
The most deadly creature on earth, the cause
of the death of an estimated one million people
each year. Sees countless hospital wards
of patients with dengue fever, malaria, the Zika virus.

Researcher closes the files, wonders about a career
in journalism. Or politics.

Contrasting Perspectives

Outskirts of a country town,
raucous rasp emerges
from the scribbly sapling.
Pale feather ends profiled
against the late afternoon light.
The grey cockatoo, scarlet head and crest,
crunches the buds.
A wasteful shower of seeds
from a wilful child.

Face reddening, the man
shakes his rake.
As though attacking
leaves in the air,
prods at the parrot.
Loose deep wing beats
as it swoops away
on the downdraught.

In the city, remembrance
of a bush reserve.
Walker pauses, asks
'Have you seen the gang-gang?'
'No, not for three weeks now.'
Shakes her head, strides on
past the promotional sign.
A planned subdivision.
The drizzle descends,
languid in silk sheets.

Passes the cloth banner,
suspended between
remnant eucalypts,
'Save the gang-gangs'.

The Conservation of Ideas

The elderly grazier shifts in his seat,
stares at the television as the snake catcher
                  throws open the bag,
releases the eastern brown, slithering silence,
into remote bushland.

Reflects upon his starting days of clearing
grazing paddocks, lumping hollow logs,
                  surprised by the head
of an unwanted extra. The play's climax
comes when the villain makes his entrance.

Clear-eyed dream of a burglar disturbed
in the hayshed then sliding, gliding into
                  the innocent wood heap.
Stretched mirage docile on the sun-drenched
road; all car windows must be closed.

The papery texture of a discarded skin.
Sheltering in a rabbit hole, behind a rock,
                  hide and seek
under sheets of galvanised iron,
building materials.

A dog is bitten yelping away into the shade,
a horse shies, venomous explorer enters
                  the house,
malodorous smell of a mouse.

The farmer ponders the puzzles of old age.

The Rhythmic Ripples

The Redundant Thermometer

The early blood chills
in the milkman's fingers,
break of day.

As he endeavours to rouse,
forehead rests against the docile flank,
breath of the roan Jersey.
Epilogue to the blanketed night.

Frost envelopes the dam.
A quarter brick, propelled underarm,
slows on the icy crystal surface.
Pseudoscientific analysis, test
of the tensile strength,
the varnished glaze, as the sun
steals above the treeline.

Many hours later at noon, the calibrated
weight still resists immersion.
Precision instrument.

Demonstrates his hypothesis,
frigid Fahrenheit.
Hands plunged in his pockets;
a glacial day.

The Kelpie's Chain

From the outlying paddock to the farmhouse,
the midnight walk of the ashen sky.
The child inches ahead, absorbs the blank fog.
No moon, no metaphor.

His body's extremities unattached,
phrases become elusive.
He shrinks from water holes conjured in the ink,
conceives the laceration of the intruding
barbed-wire fence.
The unseen fox slinks away in the darkness,
pursues the targeted lamb.

Boy scours the pitch-black
for the breath, the impassive presence, unmoving,
of the Friesian milking cow.
The inspired allegory, to create
the sustained allusion.

Dislocated, an extended trek,
vigilant ears guided by the restless rattle,
the strain of the kelpie's chain;
the homestead appears
in its distant light.

The Straining Rowlocks

An ageing man, you sip your coffee at the café wall;
the estuary is out of sight but, like a monk meditating,
you immerse yourself in the mantra
of the rowlocks, the river's rusty gates.

Your mind merges with the current and you know that
the oarsman reaches his wrists, heaves against the running tide.
The pier moans to the surge of the stream and you absorb
the yammering of the shipwright's winch.

You recollect a life of muckin' about in boats,
recall secluded days submerged, the technique
of catching fish with bait. You imagine a reverent selection
of the sharpest barbed hook.

You weight it with a split shot sinker suitable
for the flow; you cast, sew the needle
and thread with precision into the quivering quilt,
your frame braced low in the sanctity of ritual.

With flexed fingers you tighten the line pressure,
grip the cork firmly with the other hand.
In the brushstrokes of the washed watercourse
the wind lifts the rhythmic ripples,

the eddy of memory; nearby mooring ropes buckle,
yachts bounce in balance. Absorbed anticipation
seated on the gleam of fluid diamonds and then the jagged tug,
repeated as you allow the line to set.

When the bream is landed, slapping tail and spicy smell,
its gills leak reddish brine around your bare toes.
A pitching curtain of seagulls circles
your sanctuary, wheels away your furies

and your griefs up the stained-glass cliffs.
At the end the estuarine slime slides sideways
from the anchor as you haul it across the gunwale,
square your shoulders for the row home.

Decades of memories; you search for yourself in the slam,
the smack of the straining rowlocks.
It is time to request the bill.

From the Killing Tree

When its throat has been slashed,
the beast is winched up by its hind legs,
ascends the killing tree.

The carcass must be allowed to bleed,
a gush then a trickle, before being
skinned and dressed.

The sibilance of the hauling pulley in the dawn still;
every sheep dog strains at the chain,
drools in its kennel, shed.

Each eyes the gutting, yowls and yelps.

Only the man is squeamish.
Sour stench of a primal place,
acerbic astringency.

The offcuts of tomorrow.
Even highly trained dogs cannot be taught
delayed gratification.

Villanelle for Archie

The riverside arena's swathed in green.
Precocious talent as the runs flow free,
your Test debut the best they've ever seen.

Selected for Australia as a teen,
in Adelaide you make a century.
The riverside arena's swathed in green.

The greatest Englishmen bowl fast and mean.
The critics to a man can all agree,
your Test debut the best they've ever seen.

From Larwood you score runs like a machine;
delightful style, you flaunt your artistry.
The riverside arena's swathed in green.

Your tragic death could not have been foreseen,
in youth's cortege no synchronicity.
Your Test debut the best they've ever seen.

We wonder what in time you could have been,
dismissed from life when aged just twenty-three.
The riverside arena's swathed in green,
your Test debut the best they've ever seen.

Archie Jackson, 1909–1933, played test cricket for Australia,
making a century on debut aged nineteen. He died of tuberculosis.

Glinting Barrels

Warm fluid jets, squirts through praying palms,
practised fingers, a sunrise stream
into the silver bucket

a whirlpool froths between
the milkman's clenched knees.
Forehead melded to the musty flank

dank odour of the Jersey cow.
Grasshoppers sizzle on the grill of summer.
A cross-cut saw of cockatoos

skates across the dawn;
a billow of birds embroiders
the eastern sky.

News intones, cultured tones
of the BBC. Reports of defeat, retreat.
And now we have to worry about Japan.

Two brothers in north Africa; a test of his faith.
In his imagination rivulets of sweat, saturated slouch hats
bob across the sandy wastes.

On the trip to town freckled hands, exposed, melt
into the steering wheel, jeep jolts through potholes neglected
since before the war. At the top of the lane

he pauses to pick up the itinerant shearer
for weekly military training, they'll do their bit,
the Volunteer Defence Corps.

On the football oval standard-issue boots crack
the twigs as they exercise through the windblown leaves
of the half-forward flank.

Pungency of working men and materiel
engulfed by the odour of another essential service,
the abattoir drifting on the nor-easter.

The fox shooter instructs,
motor mechanic demonstrates,
hands soaked with yesterday's oil stains.

Charcoal barrels of ancient 303s
glint in the rays of the solar flare.
The government will mobilise

muster the nation against the threat;
for now the drone is not of aeroplanes
but of battalions of flies.

Trained to operate searchlights scanning
the skies. The mournful battle cry of crows.
Oh God, our help in ages past.

Rattles back to the homestead,
to the grind of rural production.
Yap, yap of border collies

backfiring retort of the tractor
replaces the rat-tat-tat of the mind.
Time to repair the scarifier

manipulates the drum rods,
clips with makeshift serrated pliers.
Yet will I fear no evil.

A Letter to Bath

The horse-drawn coach will transport
the letter to Bath on the same day.
Mud will splatter, spoked wheels
grind, running boards will jolt.
The seep of dank fog on the high
road to the west of London.
She adjusts her bonnet, silk ribands and satin smooth to her
touch. Damask teases at her brow. Parchment quivers under
the flow of the quill, face contorts as she forms the swirls,
the loops and curls. She contemplates the placement of each
word: *Dear Sister… Ever your loving.* Evaluates, calculates
the empty portion on the top right of the envelope, the space
remaining vacant to affix a newly pressed Penny Black.

Issued in Great Britain in 1840, the Penny Black was the world's
first adhesive postage stamp.

Colour Within Colour

The Sock Knitter, Grace Cossington Smith (1915), Art Gallery of New South Wales

The sitter gazes downward, immersed in her work,
her eyes escape us; extended lithe fingers
ply the needles, an unchanging click, barely audible,
of domesticity. Black hair and a mauve cardigan,
womanly on the chiffon settee.

The young artist depicts her younger sister,
the sock knitter. Face of self-contained
restraint masks the passion soaring beyond the studio,
Turramurra garden, to support the boys. Her mouth
conveys the fear and dread for absent vitality.

Bright broad brushstrokes, short and squat,
delineate form, a jigsaw of echoes;
in the words of the artist, colour within colour.

A symbol, a tribute to every unknown woman
contrasting with the tales of male heroism.
She contributes, she sits and knits.

'acclaimed as the first post-impressionist painting to be exhibited in Australia': Art Gallery of New South Wales

The Curve of Her Shoulder

Someone left the cake out in the rain
– 'MacArthur Park', Jimmy Webb (1968)

He daydreams of that day of teenage love, the city park,
before the times of angst about tomorrow.

Muted sound except her gentle breath, innocence,
caresses the curve of her shoulder in the warming sun.

Couples stroll, inhale and stroke the roses;
the tableau of a wedding party.

A dewy glaze, the severed scent of shaved grass
and soaring fragrance, the possibilities, of frangipani

sighing in the buoyant salty air. Eastern rosellas prattle
in Moreton Bay figs. The vision is *melting in the dark*.

The traffic noise rises with the buildings,
the distant ferry speeds away from its wake.

Back then he was a miniaturist, absorbed the clarity
of every bloom; *I'll never have that recipe again.*

Weeping Guitar

For George Harrison (1943–2001)

Imagine a rangy young mop top on lead guitar,
dream the virtuoso licks of a scouser;
he is flanked by more esteemed bandmates,
all in tailored suits, pointed black shoes.
When they were the fab four,
except for mothers of teenage girls.

Visualise the baby face
at the centre of that famous rock band.
Take into your pores, absorb
the pings of the Fender strings,
the chord progressions and harmonies.
Inhale the heaving hysteria,
your toes tapping to the soundtrack of the 60s.
But you will detect the reserve of a kid
uptight in the limelight.

By now you will awaken memories of 'Something'
and you will be humming the riff of
'While My Guitar Gently Weeps'.
Picture the days of longer hair,
the moustache of the disciple of mysticism,
spiritualism on a sitar, who brought Indian
classical influences to the west.

And when you are reminded of his death so young
you will be transported back to the tribute concert,
to the acclaim of his musical friends,
to his renaissance, encore as Dhani.
You will come to understand the lack of pretension,
the generosity of a reticent songwriter and vocalist,
to understand the essence of George.

Fibres of Filament

Corrugated Tymbals

The male cicada, fastened to an acacia twig,
escalates his thrum, antennae tremble.
Abdominal tymbals, corrugated, vibrate drumlike.
Joined by his rivals in unison, the chorus intensifies,
now a cacophony, then fades away into silence.
Insistent suitor persists, makes his pitch again.

A relentless pursuit, the merciless competition
for a mate. The black prince, rarity in the region,
strives to preserve, to prolong his genes.

Wandering in the park, a youthful collector
searches for a winged trophy,
imagines it pulsing in his palm.
Showpiece for the schoolyard.
He peers at a spider's web; adhesive fibres
of filament float in the midday glare.
Gossamer threads, suspended industry and menace,
have ensnared a leaf, a beetle.
And a lustrous prize.

The cicada's compound eyes deadened,
his plaintive entreaty has subsided.
Fragile lifespan of a few weeks scythed,
truncated in nature's scramble for survival.

Raptor Banquet

Fire has scorched the oat crop stubble,
adjoining yellow box saplings engulfed, overwhelmed

razing a blazing swath; sheets of flame now stall
on the depleted breeze as daylight fades.

A black kite, chevrons flaring, with easy grace
pounces on a smouldering stick

snatches the twig, swoops
and relinquishes the fire torch

in a section of unburnt foliage, the undergrowth
of the canopied scrubland.

Soars to its observation post; the panicked flush,
the squeal of possums and mice,

a harvest festival for birds of prey.

Migration of the Bar-tailed Godwits

You scour and scrounge across the tidal flats
to fortify for savage days at sea,
fatiguing flight through trackless habitats;
you probe with needle beak among the scree.
A time to wade, to sift the shrinking tide
for protein foods, a rich invertebrate,
prepare to halve your weight, the salt-wild ride,
prepare and prime to scrap and navigate.
From Hen and Chicken Bay, the urban sprawl,
you battle squalls and blizzards as you soar
across the wash, the cruel Alaska haul,
exhausted when at last you reach the shore.
You venture way beyond your hemisphere
for you must breed; you strive and persevere.

Ephemeral Pelicans

A rim-like ring, the floating foam
flows up the beach; we know it must.
Escapes the swell, separates
from the surf, cream from the milk,
glides over the candied honeycomb
of the sand.

The beaks of the pelicans,
angled like artist's brushes
on the viscous canvas,
bounce in the blackness,
an aqueous dance on the incoming tide.

An epiphany. The pelican pair drifts
into the half-light; then they paddle,
ebb away, the instant destroyed,
consumed by the night.

Soldered Strands

In the luminance from the veranda, the golden orb
                weaving spider
            sketches her
      upright script, calligraphy of the wild air

with her pointed pencil. Her contract with nature is to
        design and construct
        a puzzle
        a golden sheen to deceive, ensnare.

I watch as she line dances, clambers on the silk
        staircase,
        suspending
     her quilted handicraft to scale, adhesive

demonstration that the thinnest thread can be
        the finest rope.
        Now she hides,
    lies in wait, lemon-banded legs in the melaleuca

as if to conserve energy for another
        last waltz
        tomorrow.
     In the canted light before dawn

I wake to inspect the aftermath of all that industry,
        ambushed prey
        of moths,
    entangled, wrapped in soldered strands.

In the silence preceding the audible day,
        beauty meets terror.

Dead Tree Cycle

The ringbarked blackbutt stands stolid
in the midday glare, emaciated arms
stationary as if to confront the heat.
The globe at its zenith, inert limbs
absorb the blaze, ramrod conductors.

The branches, kindred of the trunk,
venture to expand, extend across logs
and tussocks, as shadows uncoil
through the afternoon;
even Corriedales comprehend the shade.

Approach of dusk, a rabbit savours
tactile fronds; statues melt away
as twilight fades, the darkened bark.
A rising moon, the paddock transforms,
silhouettes exhale the hours of the night.

A cemetery for trees, at dawn's
first flush the girdled ghost blooms;
pastel galahs dye the morning,
embroidered rosellas blether in cohesive pairs.
A daily rhythmic cycle.

Elevated Insight

She crouches at the upstairs window,
sun's warmth teases tensed ears.
Detects the contrasting scents,
speculates on specific stimulants,
sights and sounds of the early morning.
Monitors, evaluates.

Mass of steel shudders, screeches.
An indeterminate animal devours
its feasts, mechanical arm
rises rhythmically, crunches.

For the sentry, significance
beyond comprehension.
Disordered perspective.
Investigator assesses;
monster shrieks to our coiled
feline observer of the weekly
council truck.

Fresh Flesh

Whistling kite hovers for long hours
in search of quarry, retreats west with degradation
of the desert, the parching of rivers.

Bird of prey, blanched patchwork
on burnished bronze wings,
soars on thermal air currents.
Eerie call drifts on the updraught.
It scours, compelled to transport life
to nestlings which squeal and beg
high in the untidy blue gum nest.

In the advancing nightfall, the bird alights
on a kangaroo carcass spreadeagled
across the gravel shoulder of the road.
In statuesque silhouette, talons tear
at juicy carrion, fresh flesh.

The western glow flares
on the dust of the windscreen.
For the day's last driver there is
a sunset and a dawning:
for the raptor an endowment, a harvest.

Budding Lovers

Draped limbs of the jacarandas, blossoms
reach across the avenue. Days of fragile mauve;
brushing hands, the intimate caress of budding lovers.
Exploratory romance.

A sally of showers scuds beneath despondent sky,
invades the shade, light close-woven.
Droplets of crystal as fine as mist.

The naivety, the glow slinks, shrinks from the street,
fades to a silhouette, aftermath of memories.
Wilted leaves and crushed blooms,
a fantasy of passion now turned to slush.

Gundagai Swaths

Across the paddocks, Gundagai,
a mauve flotilla under sail.
Tableau for the highway traveller.

Seeds and shoots and suckers
spread. Across the pasture
sapphire flowers bloom,
a banquet for the bees.

Mosaic of the motorist masks
a tough winter annual,
disguises a strident survivor.
Tempting tips conceal
the iceberg, lethal lure
for hungry livestock.

Challenges the pastoralist;
to burn, to spray,
to slash.

A zephyr quivers.
The Riverina bluebell secretes
its misery. Flawed perfection
of Paterson's Curse.

A Prickly Relationship

For long periods you seem aloof,
you make no effort.

I spend so much time waiting for you,
checking on you at all hours

even at night. Our affinity appears
strained; I keep hoping you will

display your better side. There is always
a great sense of drama about you

yet you remain erect, unbending,
inflexible. Rarely, it occurs perhaps

once a year, you make a grand entrance,
laughing and preening in the middle

of the night, ostentatious and spectacular,
floral and fragrant; at last your beauty

ensures my persistence has been worthwhile.
And yet by dawn, like Cinderella

fleeing the ball, your bloom has wilted.
Queen of the night cactus.

Wavelets of Sound

A racing regatta, flotilla of sails skims,
weaves across the heads. Narrow bay
an orchestra pit crammed between
sandstone crags, each skiff integral
to the harmony of the harbour.
Syncopated energy, a symphony
composed as the concert of the wind.

Tang of salt on the tongues.
Conductor presides, pageant of gold flags
and sun-drenched buoys,
first violin leads on wavelets of sound.
Clarinets, woodwind melody,
tack on the ripples, lilt of flutes
skates across the cliffs, bass drums
sonorous against solar scarps.

Boats almost touching as though choreographed,
music soars to a crescendo,
cadence of thin cirrus clouds.
Concertmaster's strings taut on the breeze,
fleet races in unison,
the final movement now completed.

Albumen Foam

The view east, Sydney Harbour, a pellucid autumn day.
Colours refine, evolve in the sporadic sun,
erratic sky, sole constant the celadon greenwood,
a glaze fastened as lichen to the city's sandstone sunwalls.
Cumulus cloud blankets, ash grey,
caress bleached sheets.

Translucent ripples carry the scene to us here
on the deck. The spreading angophora towers,
lavender leaves as patterned curtains against
the shimmering sky. On the distant bridge
a train in miniature, civic centipede, creeps across
in silence, disappears into the North Sydney spires.
Spanning arches soar and slice out of sight
into Balls Head Reserve.

On the wharf at our feet the blanched stanchion
hosts a squabble, a spectacle.
Little pied cormorant, spliced on the glare of the tide,
airs its wings like washing to dry, defends its domain,
confronts a white-faced heron, angular persistence.

Gunmetal tug, an aquatic moth, hauls a dismasted sloop;
the purring rivercat, bitter lime water dragon, slinks on its way.
A model ferry chugs, citrine coating an apple green waterline.
Flock of boats; each flits as swallows and swifts sweep, skim.
Gulls spin and swerve, tease at albumen foam,
wheel on the sunlit flare of an anchored ketch.

In the foreground a runabout Cockatoo Hire
cuts as a knife, slides into the jetty;
the fluorescent orange workman, both driver and passenger,
pores over his phone, clinks from the end of his working week.

Alone In the Azure

Legacies of the Delta

Cheeks contort, forehead furrows,
shoulders shake and sway.
Face a sheen of sweat
as the harmonica yowls,
insistent digits dance,
drive across the guitar.
Blind man of the Depression wails
the acoustic blues.
Lacerated musicality.

A generation later, between concerts,
door opened by a chauffeur,
white man climbs from his limousine.

Searches between the unmarked graves
for the memorial for which he has paid.
For the fresh soil, luminous gravestone
shining in the sun
of the late afternoon.

Rolling Gravy Mince

In the semi-trailer cabin coasting towards the line of elms,
the driver daydreams the tang of anticipation, the taste
of town.
The best pies in Australia.

From the spherical cashier the townspeople loop
to the slamming fly screen door, scrutinise the
wire shelving,
the choice of daybreak loaves.

Scramble for the array of cakes and papery pastries.
Beneath the awning, the truckie unbends;
rolling gravy mince
oozes across the oil soaked finger

down the uniform, blue singlet and heavy leather boots.
Aroma of crusty dough, scent of burnt sugar,
dominates, overpowers the sweat of work,
the sibilant diesel rig,
wheezing inertia in the shade.

Rural hamlet; community crossroads;
refuelling stop for truckies.

Sibling Harmony

A round conference table,
the lawyer's face creases concern,
absorbs the throb, temple tension
of his client's high forehead.

A mauve scarf of hope,
incessant shoe jiggles on the carpet.
Perfume restrained yet unavoidable
in their professional proximity.

Fingers flex around the soaked sphere
of tissue, a balled Linus blanket,
right elbow angular on the blond oak.
Again the tears flow:
I was estranged from my father
but I did not expect he would leave
the lot to my sister.
Her tentative voice frets,
thin in the formal air.

The lawyer's calm voice of authority:
You may have to sue.
Your case seems strong but
is family unity important to you?

The stare of her eyes,
an effort to appear detached.
Shoulders sag, droop with the weight
of family history. She stands to leave:
I cannot believe he has done this to me.
I shall need to think about it;
I'll call you.

Orbiting the Orb

For Michael Collins on the fiftieth anniversary

Blasted by a thrust transcending our imagination,
you are impelled from Florida out beyond the distant sky.
I am one of the six hundred million particles

who peer at you from offices, from restless school assembly halls.
As commanding pilot, you set down your co-venturers to explore,
to probe the moonscape, while you orbit the orb

thirty times alone in the azure, gaze at bleak craters,
at cobalt spaces. You endure eternities of no
communication with Mission Control

or with your celestial colleagues.
Accompanied by thoughts of isolation,
the silence of your solitude, you soar

on an odyssey through the dark side of the mind.
A rocket man in a *tin can*, you learn about yourself
while others learn about the conformation of the moon.

Involuntary Witness

After the day procedure, I yawn
near the glare of the wide-angle window.
My brain still floats on the light sedation,
steaming cup of bronze tea,
tomato and cheese sandwich.
I observe the nurses bustling in
sensible shoes, attentive faces.

A middle aged woman, ash grey hair,
is wheeled past, reassuring resonance,
calm tone of the specialist.
An odour of hospital antiseptic,
tart tang of linoleum cleanser.
I adjust the dangling cord
of my surgical gown.

The professional voice again in the fractured air:
I hope that I can get it all but you will need
chemotherapy after the operation.

Silence beyond the archway,
then at last the barely audible
sighs of weeping.

Sifted

The dainty teapot arrives, delicacy of the glazed china.
She celebrates the lilting tinkle, the muted melody.
Cadence of the crockery, sonata of the spoons.

Twirls the teapot, blends the brew,
concentrates and contemplates. Inhales the fragrance,
fine leaves; reverie of the scented steam.

Ruminates on the ritual, embraces the tradition.
Memories seep as through a spout,
through a strainer of reminiscence, retrospection.
Filtered by the veil of imperfect recollection.

Oasis of calm; for a moment, an instant,
her worries have faded, vanished.

She is alone, exempted from the dialogue
of the taking of a toast and tea
and from the dangling conversation.

Viewfinder

Pixels and aperture conjure
a single black and white still.

Random incidents integrated
by the imagination
of a street photographer.

Bearded veteran, on his haunches, stares.
Tatty blanketed,
lonely shopping trolley.

A second scene is juxtaposed.
White veil on black suit,
bridal couple dashes.

Through an urban lens,
imprinted memory card.
Shutter clicks and closes;
eye opens.

Contemporary Kant

Something to do, someone to love, something to hope for
– Immanuel Kant (1724–1804)

Parka soiled, burnt coffee blanket
crumpled on the greatcoat.
Greasy hair, entangled face of fatigue.
She could be sixty. Or sixteen.
Raw breeze gusts through the arcade.

Perhaps her dog, spreadeagled, was a border collie,
now ghosted charcoal.
Bred long ago to round up lambs
far from this city precinct.

Pedestrians flock, sheep in silence,
the blast, the blare of traffic;
a savour of the streets,
of grit-glazed concrete.
Her face a blank page
but the book has been written.
Someone to love; defeated hand,
hardened, strokes the dog.

Stooping to drop some coins;
if I don't help,
the dog might die.

Postmodern Communication

The beach café, her eyes gaze down,
hair dances a tango in the fresh sea breeze.
The tang of espresso,
the brace of salt spray.

His face turned away, concentrates;
wind strokes four-day stubble.
The sound of waves crashes up from the sand,
dachshund spreadeagled beneath them.

Hushed languor? Companionable silence?
Each stares at the glare
of a mobile phone.

Flickering Flaneur

after Frank O'Hara

I step from the train just before 12 noon
on a Monday in September. An overcast sky
but there is no drizzle so I can walk
without my umbrella to deliver the envelope
to the Opera House. The box office person seems familiar.

From the bearded vendor in the paper kiosk
I buy both the *Herald* and the *Australian*
to read in Café Lucca on Castlereagh.
Fettuccine and a glass of pinot grigio;
the waiter is younger than my son.
The national news dispiriting,
our leaders arguing as ever.

The Scots continue to agitate to leave the UK,
Nicola Sturgeon's face determined in the photo.
In New York the mayor is concerned about security
for the commemoration on the Hudson
but that will be tomorrow our time;
impossible to believe it is sixteen years.

And I remember the start of the 10.30 news,
the TV flickering in the half-dark of the bedroom
as I grabbed my dressing gown, padded downstairs.
Wide-awake for the next four hours, transfixed.
This is not a movie; how many more airliners?

In the early morning hours
in theory it is time for sleep.

I'm a Celebrity Get Me Out of Syria

Too bored to read and resistant to sleep,
you flick on the television.

In Washington the President, false flick of hair,
is flanked by heads from the fairground, nodding.
He stares, announces the withdrawal
from Syria of the troops; a tiny contingent
will stay. 'We have won against ISIS.'

Eyelids drooping, you make an effort to concentrate;
analysts explain there was no consultation
with the military commander in the Middle East.
And the timeline is vague.

How to protect your neck
in the battle here on the couch?

You surf to a man in fatigues with a muddy face.
An upbeat voice implies you should care
that Shane and Dermott, former Hawthorn footballers,
will steam for three weeks in the infested jungle,
will be molested by furry-footed spiders, choreographed.
In the old style reality television, when Shane or Dermott
flew for a mark, they could perform.

Remote restless in your hand, you may tackle
the pinched Michael Mosley
on the evils of sugar.

Or another *Seinfeld* repeat. Bolstered,
or perhaps sedated, by a large glass of fine shiraz.
Or two.

Beyond Plains and Canals

The Jive of Life

The machines quarrel as they whirr and stir,
        the garments flung about in the quickstep
                of the churning foam.

A mix, a melee of customers.
        For some the washing machine at home is broken;
                some are tourists, eager to be finished;
                      some the inevitable poor.

The clients jig in the shadow dance,
        the masquerade of an English village.
                As fluoro work outfits cascade and spiral,
                      their owners shuffle, scramble
                            in a cleansing convulsion.

The clothes swirl and whirl
        in a hi-vis foxtrot,
                the people jive in the tumble,
                      the jumble of life.

Chess Pieces

Chess is life in miniature
– Garry Kasparov

Spreadeagled on garish towels,
the teenage girls on the tourist beach
are solar panels in the heat.
For their passion play they flaunt their props,
paperbacks and mobile phones.
Surf skiers drift in on languid waves,
breakers from the distant reef.

On the boardwalk the chess contestants
face off in silence. Matted hair,
dishevelled beards, tatty shirts.
Faces, fascia battered by the weather.
Holidaymakers assemble as seagulls for the showdown,
coffees donated by a spectator,
crimson lipstick and assertive sarong.

The barefoot aggressor moves his bishop,
smiles: 'Checkmate'.
His opponent surveys the sea;
for king and pawn alike the tide has run out.

Mesas and Buttes

Energetic strides, animated eyebrows,
and tweed coat, leather elbows.
Teacher of enthusiasms.

If the imagination wanders
to the oval below,
the flight is temporary.
Galvanises, jolts back
to his sphere, his dominion.
Geography.

Today it's Physical;
transported to Utah,
we visualise the unique topography
of Arid.
Winds scream off the northern prairies,
faces serrated by stark sands.
Eroded by aeolian processes,
the bitter grit of mass wasting.

Desert sagebush strives,
endures in the face of adversity.
We are schooled, stimulated
to confront the xeric days,
the seared landscapes
of mesas and buttes.

Collapsed Time

Her brother. She must see for herself, walks south, alone;
choking astringency, fetid grit of the street.
Wordless embraces, slow dances of sadness.

Firemen, rescue workers avert their eyes
from photographs, clutched.
Respectful applause, the sun glints
on dust encrusted visors.

The severance, the cleavage
of time across continents.
Purposeful but pointless, the passing of days
of twenty-four hours.
Phone calls; no news takes only seconds.
Four hundred and eighty sequential minutes
through the hours of darkness; another night.

The hospital report: on the sixth day
he was observed on a park bench
near the Hudson ferry terminal at dusk.
Eyes closed, ash covered,
streaks of what was once perspiration.
The blood from his ears was
its own narration.

Peers into her brother's eyes: Mum will be so thrilled.
Her gaze returned: tell me what I should remember
about my mother.

Looking for America

So I looked at the scenery
She read her magazine.
 – 'America', Simon and Garfunkel

A pair of blue denims, a parka, January draughts
gust through crevices, crevasses of a Greyhound,
overnight transport of the poor. Anchored in
an upright bunk, odour of the matted mass.

A month from west coast to the east,
a month of rhythmic bounce of wheels
trundling along the interstates to harmonies
of Paul Simon, his rhythmic rhyme.

At midnight we roll into Flagstaff, Arizona.
Iridescent interplay across the passengers
roused, ruffled by fleeting streetlamps,
occasional headlights of oncoming pickups.
Gritty city bus station, driver stretches,
five minutes.

We sweep along the highway, baby dozes,
'colored' section at the back.
Tattered cardigan of his mother,
she gazes out into the dark, fug of smoke.
Jaws sag, no Rosa Parks here.
Murmurs to her neighbour, Carter is from the south,
a glance of hope for the inauguration.

And the moon rose over an open field.
The lilting voice of Art Garfunkel
across the vastness of the plains of Texas.
I sway, shudder a dream against the winter window.
My deprivation is a lack of sleep.

The leg from El Paso to San Antonio,
its sixth hour, in the staleness of our thin tin can,
eyelids droop at last.
We have found America.

The Authority of Survival

His T-shirt 'No guns' appears identical to the others,
orange pastel sways before him;
teenage physique too callow for the confidence,
bravado of leadership.
As he speaks, muffled words tentative into the megaphone
die as dust within the park.

The river breeze ruffles the eager heads of hair,
smooth against the skin; like a tide students stream,
a peaceful flow, fluid across Brooklyn Bridge.
Guy ropes stir under grasping hands,
the throb of a ferry below drifts on the odour,
redolence of a creeping tanker.

While the tyres of yellow school buses sing
along the freeways back to Florida,
televisions will flicker reporting
the National School Walkout.
The pale orange-clad boy will feature,
sole survivor of the depravity of a February day.

National School Walkout, New York, 3 June 2018

An Hour at the Hermitage

Disgorged from the coach as corks extracted from a bottle,
what surprises is the queues; we enter,
squeezed through the tube. We wait for the cloakroom,
we queue for significant artworks.

Sweating bodies, we are jostled (with courtesy)
as we inch towards the magnitude
of *The Return of the Prodigal Son*.
Respectful murmur, the taste of biblical history,
the tang of high art.

Distracted by the hordes, by uniformed security,
perhaps by my imagination, the spectre of history.
I would like to step back, to take in the red, the contrasts of shades,
as we assume Rembrandt intended. Instead I am urged forward,
carried awash in a current of heads towards an excellent
perspective of the dark at the painting's right edge.

After thirty seconds it is time to shuffle as though shackled
for a glance at the *Madonna Litta*; mother's love
for a beatific child, the play of light on light.
Perhaps by Leonardo da Vinci, perhaps his pupil.
I gaze from myopic distance.

The Moderns seized from collectors remain a dream;
no Cezanne, Matisse or Picasso. As we turn to leave
I catch a glimpse of Palace Square, the weight of the Bloody
    Sunday massacre,
of the October Revolution, but we surge away and the Square
    eludes us.

Imagined Russia

Our guide, fur-lined coat, bears no resemblance
but she is Julie Christie slogging along the icy street,
the endless lilt of 'Lara's Theme'.

From the boat the soft hues of the palaces,
onion domes of cathedrals, turrets pierce and
rise out of granite embankments.

Jewels of baroque crown the narrow canals,
the apartments in slate grey,
Stalin's thorn tiaras.

We truss ourselves against the bleak,
the bitter wind and slicing rain,
shy our heads below the low bridges.

My images are of the snow and sleet, the tundra.
In silence melting icicles run as a floe down my neck.
The cowered peasants, tartaric taste of terror.

Immersed in the Revolution, yesterday though
a hundred years ago. The contrast of dejected
Soviet structures, no Amber Room here.

Commanding knock, insistent midnight knuckles on the wooden door.
The purges of the poets, the agonies of Akhmatova.
How can decades of slaughter seem so drab?

Gold filigree, figures in the fountains; the squall from the square
gusts across the floors of glacial marble, moans through
the Church of the Spilled Blood.

Our leader, tired at the last:
I am pleased to see you so happy; our children must
take school seriously, they are taught not to smile.

Coagulated Time

At first it could be any peaceful village clinging
                      to the coast, not many shops;
houses with ocean views dot,
            hold fast to the escarpment.

At the heritage wooden wharf, café chic
                    on the water's edge,
everyone goes about their business.
We scour, investigate beyond the facade
                    of appearances, the pretence of resilience.

We search in cul-de-sacs; the burnt out houses
                    and vacant blocks elude us;
          surely they have not been rebuilt.

Walls of flame sear the imagination,
                an ash-filled nightmare,
singed specks float in the scorched air
          and settle bobbing, lapping,
                the troubled sea.
A scalded possum squeals,
         the aftertaste of wildlife.
Gutted houses of the mind
         disappear in an instant.
Sooty time, condensed time coagulated;
                the blood chills in the heat.

Dwellings destroyed at random,
                the occasional one left untouched
in the residual detritus. The placid expression
          of a child's teddy, charred,
                original ears spared.

The melancholy, the hope, proliferation
of freshly green foliage sprouting
                on scarred charcoal trunks.
Houses reappear; the people may be as dust
       but they bear all things,
              endure all things.

Freight Train of the Senses

In Fremantle the railway line passes
by the waterfront cafés
and I can take in the freight train
rumbling along beside the harbour.
Sensory stimuli.

The locomotive appears, gleam of glare,
the passage of open wagons as they inch
past the boom barrier.
The water calms, tranquilises;
the engine galvanises, overawes.

The diesel fumes assault the diners,
all-encompassing invader,
surrounding reek a working, sweating
machine, rolling stock straining to hang on.
The whiff of fish and chips.

My ears soak up the grind of mechanical thrust,
the squeal of wheel to track,
the primal groan of carriage couplings
stifling, purging the circling
cry of seagulls.

I sample the aftertaste
of industrial grime at large
merged with the saline
estuarine breeze,
the tastes of our tenure.

The last oyster eaten,
it is time to approach
the pedestrian gates.

Resolutions For a Different Day

Today I shall attempt to know the peace of existing in this moment;
I shall aim to undertake a little less rather than more.
I shall avoid the negative and churlish, read and watch less news.
I shall fly with the spontaneity of the musk lorikeet
but have the forbearance to wait my turn at life's birdbath
even on the sweltering days.
I shall saunter with the silence of the diamond python
expecting that I need not gorge on life every day.
I shall learn more about the Serengeti,
the redolence of the migration, but admire,
value the tactility of the closest angophora
and understand that while travel may broaden the mind
it may not deepen it.
I shall empathise with the trials and deprivations
of the single mother and of the elderly widower.
I shall share the company of genial friends,
read history and literary fiction,
listen to music which I have not explored…
and to the Beatles (again).
I shall acknowledge that darkness arrives with every evening
and at times also during the day.
I shall endeavour to accept love and forgiveness.
I shall aspire to live with grace and peace.

Thanks

I would like to thank Ron Wilkins, Gisela Sophia Nittel and also the members of the Harbourside poetry group who provided comments and made suggestions in relation to many of the draft poems. Thanks also to the members of the Eastwood poetry group for continuing support in the exploration of poetry.

My loving appreciation to Judy for her constant support as always.

www.ingramcontent.com/pod-product-compliance
Lightning Source LLC
Chambersburg PA
CBHW070920080526
44589CB00013B/1384